D0584969

Getting Around

By Train

Cassie Mayer

PETERBOROUGH LIBRARIES	
9736	
Bertrams	26.05.07
J385	£9.50
	✓

www.heinemann.co.uk/library
Visit our website to find out more information about **Heinemann Library** books.

To order:
 Phone 44 (0) 1865 888066
 Send a fax to 44 (0) 1865 314091
Visit the Heinemann Bookshop at www.heinemann.co.uk/library to browse our catalogue and order online.

First published in Great Britain by Heinemann Library, Halley Court, Jordan Hill, Oxford OX2 8EJ, part of Harcourt Education. Heinemann is a registered trademark of Harcourt Education Ltd.

© Harcourt Education Ltd 2006.
The moral right of the proprietor has been asserted.

All rights reserved. No part of this publication may be reproduced, stored in a retrieval system, or transmitted in any form or by any means, electronic, mechanical, photocopying, recording, or otherwise, without either the prior written permission of the publishers or a licence permitting restricted copying in the United Kingdom issued by the Copyright Licensing Agency Ltd, 90 Tottenham Court Road, London W1T 4LP (www.cla.co.uk).

Editorial: Tracey Crawford, Cassie Mayer, Dan Nunn, and Sarah Chappelow
Design: Jo Hinton-Malivoire
Picture Research: Tracy Cummins
Production: Duncan Gilbert

Originated by Chroma Graphics (Overseas) Pte. Ltd
Printed and bound in China by South China Printing Company

10 digit ISBN 0 431 18221 3
13 digit ISBN 978 0 431 18221 6

10 09 08 07 06
10 9 8 7 6 5 4 3 2 1

British Library Cataloguing in Publication Data
Mayer, Cassie
Getting around by train
1.Railroad travel - Juvenile literature 2.Railroads - Juvenile literature
I.Title
385

Acknowledgements
The publishers would like to thank the following for permission to reproduce photographs:
Corbis pp. **4** (Royalty Free), **5** (Svenja-Foto/zefa), **6** (Catherine Karnow), **7** (Colin Garratt/Milepost $92^{1/2}$), **8** (John Garrett), **9** (Dave G. Houser), **10** (Colin Garratt/Milepost $92^{1/2}$), **11** (Colin Garratt/Milepost $92^{1/2}$), **12** (Jack Fields), **13** (Joseph Sohm/ChromoSohm Inc), **14** (José Fuste Raga/zefa), **15** (Tom Bean), **16** (Jose Fuste Raga), **17** (James L. Amos), **18** (Goebel/zefa), **19** (Gerald French), **20** (Munish Sharma/Reuters), **21** (Rick Gomez), **22** (Douglas Peebles), **23** (Colin Garratt/Milepost $92^{1/2}$), **23** (Joseph Sohm/ChromoSohm Inc.), **23** (Jack Fields), **23** (Colin Garratt/Milepost $92^{1/2}$).

Cover image of a steam train reproduced with permission of Dave G. Houser/Corbis. Back cover image of an interurban train reproduced with permission of Svenja-Foto/zefa/Corbis.

Every effort has been made to contact copyright holders of any material reproduced in this book. Any omissions will be rectified in subsequent printings if notice is given to the publishers.

The paper used to print this book comes from sustainable resources.

Contents

Getting around by train

Every day people move from place to place.

Some people move by train.

What trains carry

Some trains carry passengers.

Some trains carry cargo.

How trains move

wheel

Trains have wheels.

track

The wheels move on tracks.

Trains have an engine.
An engine can push the train.

An engine can pull the train.

Who works on trains?

driver

A train driver drives the train.

conductor

A conductor helps passengers on the train.

Where trains go

Trains go up mountains.

Trains go along cliffs.

Trains go across cities.

Trains go across the country.

Trains go over bridges.

Trains go through tunnels.

Trains can take you to many places.

And trains can
take you home.

Train vocabulary

coach

engine

wheel

track

Picture glossary

 **cargo** things taken from one place to another

 **conductor** the person who helps people on board the train

 **track** what train wheels ride on

 **train driver** the person who drives the train

Index

Notes to Parents and Teachers

Before reading

Talk about going on a train journey. Where did they go? Where did they sit? What did they see? Talk about the engine, the wheels, the tracks, and tunnels. Talk about people who work on trains: the driver and the conductor.

After reading

Tell the children to pretend to be trains. They should use their arms to be the pistons. Talk about how a train starts slowly as it pulls out of the station and then it gets faster.
Say this rhyme as they move, getting faster and faster: Coff - ee, Coff - ee, Cheese and biscuits, Cheese and biscuits, Plums and custard, Plums and custard, Fish and chips, Fish and chips, Soooooooup.
Tell the children the train is going through a tunnel. They will have to crawl on their hands and knees.
Role play "Going on a train journey". Act out buying a ticket, waiting on the platform, getting on board, and looking out of the window.

Titles in the *Getting Around* series include:

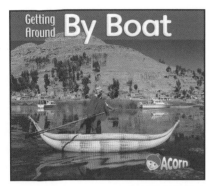

Hardback   0-431-18222-1

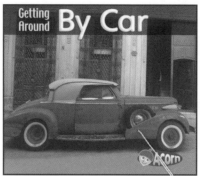

Hardback   0-431-18218-3

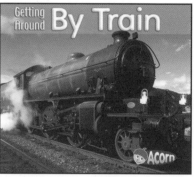

Hardback   0-431-18221-3

Hardback   0-431-18216-7

Hardback   0-431-18217-5

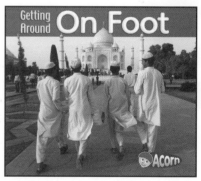

Hardback   0-431-18219-1

Find out about other titles from Heinemann Library on our website www.heinemann.co.uk/library